TRADITIONAL SCOTTISH FOOD

Meg Cowie

Chambers

Published by W & R Chambers Ltd Edinburgh, 1989
Reprinted 1989, 1990

British Library Cataloguing in Publication Data
Cowie, Meg
  Traditional Scottish Food.—
  (Chambers mini guides).
  1. Food. Scottish dishes. Recipes
  I. Title
  641.59411

  ISBN 0-550-20055-X

Cover design by John Marshall

Typeset by Bookworm Typesetting Ltd, Edinburgh
Printed in Singapore by
Singapore National Printers Ltd

Contents

*Except where otherwise stated all recipes
are to serve four people.*

Preface

Scotland is famous throughout the world for its haggis and neeps, black bun and shortbread, but there are many other traditional Scottish dishes for you to enjoy. Scotch broth, for instance, makes a fine and warming start to any meal; stovies a quick standby and tablet a sweet treat.

The Scots are renowned as a nation of travellers and many foreign recipes will almost certainly have been changed or developed by them as they travelled round the world. At the same time many people far from Scotland will be familiar with the customs and food associated with St Andrew's Night, Burns Night and Hogmanay.

This book introduces the best known traditional Scottish food and gives easy-to-follow instructions on how to produce good results using today's modern cookery methods.

Meg Cowie

The Selkirk Grace

Some hae meat and cannae eat,
And some wad eat that want it:
But we hae meat and we can eat
Sae let the Lord be thankit.

Burns

Equipment

This book aims to give a modern approach to traditional Scottish cookery so that you can enjoy the flavour of Scotland at its best. Most of the equipment mentioned in the recipes is in general use in most kitchens. Of course, not all recipes use all pieces of equipment: some dishes lend themselves to gentle stewing in a slow-cooker, while others are better in a pressure cooker.

However the main pieces of equipment used in the preparation of the recipes are as follows:

A good kitchen knife
This is an invaluable tool. It is too easy to assume that whatever knife is available will 'do' for the job. A medium-sized blade which will cut everything from neeps to the most delicate of chives is absolutely essential.

A good chopping board
There is no substitute for a good hardwood chopping board. On this you can chop vegetables, cut meat or roll flour and at the same time save your work top.

A spurtle (or a wooden spoon)
A spurtle is a wooden spoon without the wide spoon shape at the end. In effect, it is a piece of wood with a rounded end. Traditionally it was used for stirring porridge but, of course, it can also be put to work stirring soups, oatcake mixes and stews.

A girdle
A girdle is a flat pan used on top of the cooker and is a close relative of the curved Chinese wok. It

was traditionally made of cast iron for use over an open fire. Modern girdles can be used on top of an ordinary electric or gas cooker, or indeed heated over a ceramic hob.

Slow-cooker, microwave cooker and pressure cooker
The modern cook can combine traditional recipes with modern technology to produce a perfect 'traditional' meal. You need only be familiar with your equipment to be able to adopt traditional recipes to suit the demands of the twentieth century.

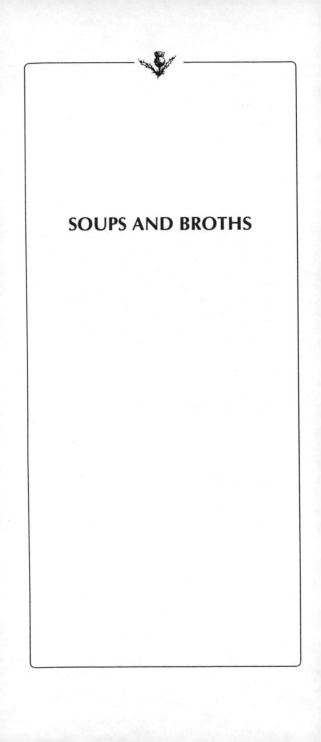

SOUPS AND BROTHS

Basic Stock

Scottish housewives are famous for their soup throughout the world. This is because they have not forgotten how to make the basic stock that is an essential part of any soup recipe. You can make the best stock from a ham bone, a cut of boiling beef, or from a chicken carcass; or you can use the stock that is left in jelly form from boiling or roasting a chicken or a joint of ham (the dripping that is left from roasting beef is best used for stovies).

The soups here all freeze well – it is a good idea to freeze the soup in individual portions so that those who want soup can take their own portion out of the freezer and defrost it within minutes in the microwave. For single people and those who entertain on the spur of the moment, it makes having guests very easy.

Stock using bones is best made in the pressure cooker, but excellent stock can also be made on the top of the cooker. Whichever method you use, the ingredients are the same, only the cooking time varies. Metric and imperial weights are only approximately equivalent.

Ingredients

ham shank, chicken carcass *or* boiling beef
1 onion
1 carrot
a few pieces of rough cut celery
1 litre (2 pints) water

Method

Place all the ingredients in a heavy-based pot. Bring to the boil and simmer on the top of the cooker for about an hour, or at full pressure for 15 to 20 minutes. Discard the vegetables.

Chicken and beef stock usually need salt added to taste, but be careful with ham stock – it can be very salty to start with.

Scotch Broth

Ingredients

beef stock made up to 1 litre (2 pints) with
    water
handful of 'broth mixture', which is easily
    bought in a supermarket
    or
    handful of dried green peas, dried mixed
    vegetables, and (optional) barley
1 sliced leek
handful of chopped kale
2 chopped onions
2 grated carrots

Method

Place all the ingredients in a pot or pressure
cooker and bring to the boil. Simmer for
about an hour, or cook at full pressure for
20 minutes. This soup does not work well in
the microwave or slow-cooker because of
the dried ingredients.

Serve on a cold winter's day, or to visitors
just before they get on their way into the
night.

Lentil Soup

Ingredients

ham stock made up with water to 1 litre (2 pints)
150 g (6 oz) lentils (or yellow split peas)
3 cleaned and grated carrots
2 cleaned and finely chopped onions
2 leeks
salt and pepper to taste

Method

Put all the ingredients except the leeks into a pot or pressure cooker. Bring to the boil and simmer for an hour on top of the cooker, or cook for 15 minutes at full pressure in a pressure cooker. Ten minutes before serving, add the finely chopped leeks.

This is a delicious soup for winter, and makes a perfect lunch when served with bread and cheese, or toasted cheese and onion. Do not try to make it in the slow-cooker or microwave – the lentils do not 'mush down' properly.

Tattie Soup
(potato soup)

Ingredients

ham or chicken stock made up to 1 litre (2 pints)
1 kg (2 lb) peeled and rough chopped potatoes (the floury varieties are better)
2 medium rough chopped onions
2 to 3 pieces of rough chopped celery
2 rough chopped leeks
1 dessertspoon mashed potato mix to thicken
salt and pepper to taste

Method

Put the potatoes, onions, celery and stock into a pot and bring to the boil for about 20 to 25 minutes (10 minutes in the pressure cooker at full pressure). Remove from the heat and blend in a food processor or liquidiser. Stir in the potato powder, seasoning and the leeks. You can add a drop of milk or cream at this stage, but if you do, ensure that it does not boil when you are reheating it.

Instead of using a blender, you can mash down the vegetables with a potato masher for a rougher but equally delicious soup which retains pieces of potato.

Cock-a-leekie
(chicken & leek soup)

Ingredients

chicken stock made up to 1 litre (2 pints) with
   water
handful of rice
1 finely chopped onion
3 finely chopped leeks
salt and pepper to taste

Method

Cock-a-leekie is a very tasty and quick soup
to make. Twenty minutes on top of the
cooker, or 15 minutes at full power in the
microwave will see it ready, so it really is not
worth using a pressure cooker. Alternatively,
you can put all the ingredients in the slow-
cooker, and leave it to cook for about 6
hours while you do something else.

Chicken Broth

Ingredients

chicken stock made up to 1 litre (2 pints) with
    water
2 large or 3 medium-sized grated carrots
2 medium onions, chopped finely
50 g (2 oz) broth mixture
salt and pepper to taste
2 finely chopped leeks

Method

Put all the ingredients except the leeks into a large pot or pressure cooker. Bring to the boil and simmer for 1 to 1½ hours on the top of the cooker, or 15 to 20 minutes at full pressure. Add the leeks 10 minutes before serving.

Like all soups containing pulses, chicken broth does not cook well in the slow-cooker or microwave.

Nettle Soup

Ingredients

chicken stock made up to 1 litre (2 pints) with
    water
1 kg (2 lb) of young nettles, freshly picked
    from a country lane or forest
handful of rice
2 dessertspoons mashed potato mix to
    thicken
salt and pepper to taste

Method

Put the chopped nettles, stock and rice in a
pot. Bring to the boil and simmer for 15
minutes. Remove from the heat and blend in
a food processor or liquidiser. Stir in the
mashed potato and season to taste.

Serve with oatcakes and caboc for a
satisfying and unusual meal.

Barley Broth

Ingredients

1 litre (2 pints) stock from beef or lamb
250 g (8 oz) barley
handful or so of dried green peas
2 grated carrots
quarter of a turnip, skinned and grated
1 diced potato
1 finely chopped onion
2 finely chopped leeks

Method

Put all the ingredients into a pot and bring to the boil. Simmer on the top of the cooker for just over an hour, or until the peas are as soft as you like them. (A lot of people like them quite chewy).

Serve hot with crusty bread, or with morning rolls filled with left-over mince.

Barefit Broth

Barefit broth (or 'bare-foot' broth) is a cheaper version of traditional soup because it contains no stock other than water. Stock is so inexpensive to make from the remnants of other dishes, however, that few people nowadays would base their soup on water.

Ingredients

250 g (8 oz) barley
3 grated carrots
2 finely chopped onions
quarter of a turnip, diced
500 g (1 lb) peeled and diced potatoes
quarter of a cabbage finely chopped
1½ litres (3 pints) water
salt and pepper to taste

Method

Put all the ingredients in a pot, bring to the boil and simmer for about 1 to 1½ hours, or cook at full power in a pressure cooker for 20 minutes. Serve with oatcakes and butter.

Cullen Skink
(fish soup)

Ingredients

1 Finnan haddock
1 chopped onion
½ litre (1 pint) milk
mashed potatoes *or* mashed potato mix
25 g (1 oz) butter
salt and black pepper to taste

Method

Place the fish in a pot and just cover it with water. Bring to the boil, add the onion and then simmer for about 5 minutes until the fish is poached through. Remove the fish from the pot, flake off all the flesh and retain it. Meanwhile, put the bones back in the stock, and simmer this gently for another 30 minutes. Strain off the stock into a fresh pot, add the milk and flaked fish, making sure that the soup does not boil. Add enough mashed potato or potato mix to make a nice creamy soup. Season, and add the butter just before serving.

Partan Bree
(crab soup)

Ingredients

Take the meat from one crab, and retain the claw meat. Alternatively, you can cheat by using a large tin of crab meat, retaining the larger flakes for garnish.
250 g (8 oz) rice
½ litre (1 pint) milk
½ litre (1 pint) chicken stock
salt and pepper to taste
200 ml (½ pint) cream
Anchovies (to taste) as garnish

Method

Put the milk and rice into a pot and bring to the boil. Simmer until the rice is soft, and add the flaked crab meat. Simmer for about 4 to 5 minutes, and blend in a food processor or liquidiser. Add the stock and seasoning, including a little anchovy to taste, and reheat gently.

Just before serving add the cream; garnish with the large flakes of crab meat from the claws, and some parsley or paprika.

13

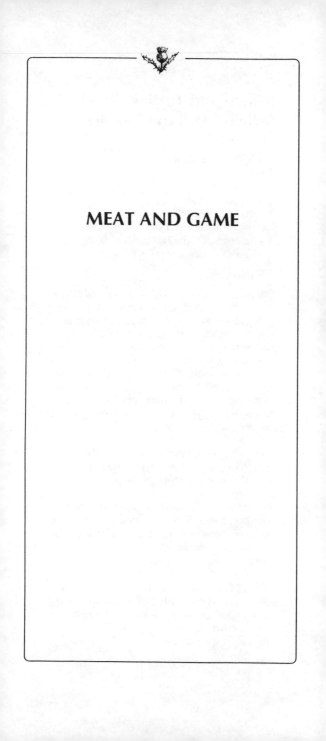

MEAT AND GAME

Mince and Tatties
(minced steak and potatoes)

Ingredients

500 g (1 lb) steak mince
2 onions
1 beef stock cube
gravy mix/thickener
2 carrots (optional)
handful of peas (optional)
1 small can of tomatoes (optional)
handful of oatmeal (optional)

Method

Brown the mince slowly over a low heat and pour off any fat that melts out of the meat. Chop the onions finely and add to the mince along with the stock cube dissolved in just under half a litre (½ pint) of boiling water. Add any optional extras now, and allow to simmer for about 20 minutes on the cooker. You can put the mince into your slow-cooker at this point, and leave it to cook for 7 hours; or into the pressure cooker for 10 minutes at full pressure.

Five minutes before serving, add the gravy mix/thickener, but watch that the gravy does not stick to the bottom of the pan.

In the meantime, wash or peel the potatoes, and boil them in salted water until they are soft, or cook them on full power in the microwave for about 15 minutes, depending on the power of your oven.

Many people like to mash up the potatoes in the mince as they eat, and a favourite relish with mince and tatties is pickled beetroot or spicy brown sauce.

Stovies
(stoved potatoes)

Ingredients

1.5 kg (3 lb) potatoes
4 sliced onions
2 cupfuls of jelly and dripping from roasting beef

Method

Rough chop the potatoes with or without their skins and place in a large pot or pressure cooker with the onions, the roast beef dripping, a little water and some salt. Boil for about 20 minutes, or 5 minutes at full pressure. Served with slices of roast beef, corned beef, or on their own, stovies make a quick and tasty meal. Some people add carrots or chopped beef before cooking.

Stovies are often served as a pub meal, but they are more popular on the east coast than the west. They do not freeze well.

Meat Loaf

Ingredients

500 g (1 lb) steak mince
100 g (4 oz) breadcrumbs
50 g (2 oz) chopped streaky bacon
1 finely chopped onion
salt and pepper to taste
pinch of English mustard powder
1 beaten egg

Method

Combine all the ingredients until they are mixed thoroughly, and pack into a meat loaf jar. Tightly seal the jar with greaseproof paper tied with string (if you are really smart you can make a handle which makes the jar easier to pick up when it is hot). Place the jar in a pot half-filled with boiling water and steam on a medium heat for 2 hours. Alternatively, pack the mixture into a rectangular microwave-proof dish and cook, uncovered, on full power for 12 minutes. (Standing time about 4 minutes).

Meat loaf is delicious served hot with a tomato-based sauce, or cold with salad, stovies or colcannon.

Forfar Bridies
(minced steak pastries)

Ingredients

Pastry:
400 g (12 oz) plain flour
a little salt
water to mix

Filling:
500 g (1 lb) browned minced beef
2 finely chopped onions

Method

Make the pastry by combining the ingredients to form a stiff paste, which you should then flour to make more manageable.

Roll out the pastry and cut into oval shapes about the size of a man's hand. Spoon on enough mince to fill half the oval and add onion to taste. Sprinkle with salt and pepper.

Wet the edges of the pastry oval, fold over and crimp the edges together. Brush the top with milk to glaze, and bake in a hot oven for about 20 minutes until the pastry is golden brown.

Bridies are delicious hot or cold, with brown or tomato sauce or chilli relish, and are great snacks for short lunch hours!

Shepherd's Pie

Ingredients

500 g (1 lb) minced steak (cooked as for mince and tatties)
or leftover mince
enough chappit tatties to form a thick topping on the mince

Method

Place the mince in a metal pie dish or ashet, so that it forms a thick layer in the base. Top either with mashed potatoes specially made for the pie, or with left-over chappit tatties. In an emergency, use mashed potato mix.

Make a pattern on top with a fork, and dot with butter.

Reheat the pie in a moderate oven, or in the microwave on a medium heat for 7 to 8 minutes.

Serve with new brussels sprouts, or chopped cabbage and onion steamed for 10 minutes and tossed in butter.

Potted Hough
(jellied shin of beef)

Ingredients

1.5 kg (3 lb) hough (shin of beef)
salt and pepper

Method

Break the bone through the middle, or into sizes which will fit into a large pot. Cover with water and bring almost to the boil. Cover with a lid, and simmer very gently for 6 to 7 hours.

When the hough is ready, the meat will come away from the bone easily. Mince the meat, and return it to the stock in the pan, adding a little water to cover it, if necessary. Season and boil for just under 10 minutes. Take it off the heat for a few minutes, then turn the mixture into moulds or bowls of a size suitable for your needs. Leave to cool.

Potted hough is lovely served with salads in summer, or on an open sandwich with a spicy or fruit sauce to garnish.

Scotch Eggs
(savoury eggs)

Ingredients

4 hard-boiled eggs
1 beaten egg
400 g (12 oz) sausage meat
breadcrumbs

Method

Dip each of the hard-boiled eggs in the beaten egg, and generously cover each egg with enough sausage meat to make a thick coating. Coat the sausage meat with the beaten egg, and roll each covered egg in breadcrumbs. Deep fry for 7 to 10 minutes.

Scotch eggs can be served hot with vegetables, or cold with salad. They are specially suitable for picnics.

Sausage Rolls

Ingredients

250 g (8 oz) flaky pastry – either home-made
   or bought frozen
500 g (1 lb) sausage meat
milk or water

Method

Roll out the pastry and cut into strips 10 cm wide and 15 cm long. Pack one side of each strip with sausage meat, season, and fold over the other half to form a roll. Seal the long end with water, and brush the top with milk.

Place all the sausage rolls on a greased baking tray, and bake in a hot oven for 15 to 20 minutes until golden brown.

You can use the same principle to make bite-sized rolls for parties by cutting strips of 5 × 30 cm (2 × 12 in.), filling them in the same way, then chopping the long sausage roll into rolls of 2 to 3 cm (1 in.). Cook in a hot oven for about 8 to 10 minutes and serve hot with drinks.

Tripe and Onions

Ingredients

500 g (1 lb) prepared tripe
3 onions
25 g (1 oz) butter
200 ml (½ pint) milk
25 g (1 oz) cornflour
salt and pepper

Method

Wash the tripe, and cut it into small pieces, along with the onions. Put these with salt and pepper into a pot and cover with boiling water. Bring to the boil and simmer for about 2½ to 3 hours (take advice from the butcher) or cook at full pressure in a pressure cooker for 50 to 60 minutes. Remove from heat, and drain.

Make a sauce by melting the butter gently in the pan with the tripe and most of the milk. Blend the cornflour with the remainder of the milk; heat the tripe and milk mixture gently, and stir in the cornflour and milk to thicken it.

Serve with parsley and black pepper.

Rabbit

Ingredients

500 g (1 lb) prepared rabbit *or* 1 rabbit from
    the butcher
2 chopped onions
2 diced carrots
some chopped green pepper
½ litre (1 pint) of beef stock

Method

Brown the rabbit lightly in a pan then add all
the other ingredients. You can gently simmer
the stew on the top of the cooker for about 40
minutes, watching that the stock does not
reduce. Alternatively, transfer the ingredients
to an oven-proof casserole dish, and cook in
a moderate oven for 45 to 50 minutes, or
longer if you turn the oven right down. Serve
with scallop potatoes.

This dish does well overnight, or for 8 hours,
in the slow-cooker; it may also be cooked at
full pressure in the pressure cooker for 25
minutes.

Venison

Venison can be cooked as a casserole in the same way as rabbit, or it can be cut into steaks and baked in a thin stock in a covered oven-proof dish. Alternatively, rub a joint of venison with oil and seasoning, and wrap it carefully in foil, making sure that there are no leakage points. Bake in a moderate oven allowing 20 minutes per pound, plus an extra 30 minutes.

Serve with a thin gravy.

Pheasant

Pheasant can be roasted in the same way as a chicken. It is a rather dry meat, so many people prefer it served with a light gravy.

Alternatively, the bird can be chopped into portions and casseroled in a light stock flavoured with a glass of red wine, which can be made into a gravy just before serving by adding a little cornflour. Season to taste, and serve with potatoes and a green vegetable or tomatoes baked in the casserole for 10 to 15 minutes.

Liver and Onions

Ingredients

100 to 150 g (4 to 6 oz) lamb's liver
1 finely chopped medium onion per person
25 g (1 oz) butter
a little oil

Method

Grill the liver for about 8 minutes each side, depending on the thickness of the cut. Melt the butter and oil in a pan and drop in the finely chopped onion. There are two ways of cooking the onions. Some people like them soft and transparent, while others like them cooked quickly so that they are brown and crispy. This is purely a matter of taste.

Serve the liver and onions with mashed potatoes — use the remainder of the butter from the pan as a sauce over the potatoes.

Many people say that pig's liver soaked in milk for about half an hour, then washed prior to cooking, is as tender as lamb's but has more flavour.

Lamb Chops
(eaten with your fingers)

Lamb is another Scottish favourite. Serve lamb chops in abundance without any trimmings. Seal the chops in a frying-pan, 2 minutes each side, then transfer to the grill where they will crisp up to perfection. This makes for an informal meal rather than an elegant occasion.

Lamb chops are also excellent when cooked on the barbecue.

Leg of Lamb

Leg of lamb can be roasted in a moderate oven in a regular roasting, self-basting tin. Allow 20 minutes per pound plus 25 to 30 minutes. Cook with the lid off for the last 20 minutes to allow the skin to crisp up. (The suet from the roasting tin can be used to make stovies.)

A more traditional way to cook lamb, however, is to bring it to the boil gently in water. Add seasoning and some carrots, and simmer with the lid on for about an hour. Serve with mashed potatoes.

Leg of lamb can also be cooked overnight in the slow-cooker, and served cold the following evening with pickles and bread and butter.

These last two methods of cooking will give you excellent stock for Scotch broth.

Aberdeen Angus Steak

No Scottish cookery book is complete without a recipe for this beef, famous throughout the world for its flavour and tenderness.

Cook the fillet and T-bone steak under the grill or in a hot frying-pan to seal in its goodness. Sirloin is just as flavoursome, but needs to be grilled or fried at a gentler heat.

For those who prefer steak well done: seal a sirloin steak in a frying-pan, 2 to 3 minutes each side, then season it with a little salt and black pepper, wrap it in foil, and cook it in a moderate oven for 25 to 30 minutes. Serve steak with onions fried transparent or brown, or with fresh or home-made bread for a delicious meal.

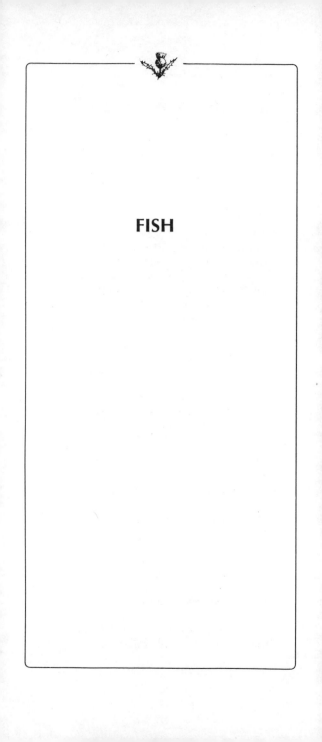

FISH

Scottish Salmon

Ingredients

whole salmon or salmon steaks
black pepper
salt
a little butter

Method

Make sure the salmon is clean then rub butter sparingly into the skin of the whole fish or dot the steaks with a little butter. The fish can be gently poached in just enough water to cover it, allowing 15 minutes per pound.

If you want to bake the fish, wrap the whole fish in foil (making sure that there are no leakage points) or place the steaks in an oven-proof glass dish and cover with foil. The fish will take about 15 minutes per pound in a moderate conventional oven, or 5 minutes per pound in a medium micro-wave. If you are using a microwave, remember to cover the tail of the salmon with foil until the last 10 minutes, since it will cook much faster than the body of the fish. The whole fish will not need to be wrapped as the skin acts as a natural cling film; a dish of salmon steaks to be cooked in a micro-wave should be covered in cling film, not foil.

Salmon steaks are ideal cooked for 7 hours in the slow-cooker covered with just enough water and a dash of milk.

Now that salmon has become a luxury dish, it seems strange to think that it was once so plentiful that it frequently formed part of farmworkers' wages and featured in the rural diet with monotonous regularity.

Enjoy it served hot or cold, with fennel and baked potatoes, or with salad.

Herring in Oatmeal

Ingredients

2 medium herring per person
handful of soft oatmeal

Method

Coat the herring with the oatmeal and fry in a little oil and butter until golden brown.

Herring should only be eaten during months that have an *R* in them, and do not react too well to the freezer. They are lovely served with boiled potatoes sprinkled with chopped parsley.

Fish in Milk

Ingredients (for two)

500 g (1 lb) smoked haddock *or* white
    haddock *or* cod
½ litre (1 pint) fresh milk
50 g (2 oz) butter
black pepper and salt to taste

Method

Heat the butter and milk on the top of the
stove or in the microwave until the mixture is
hot, but not boiling. Make sure the milk
never boils as you are cooking this dish. Add
the fish and cook gently for about 5 minutes
in a pot or 4 to 6 minutes on medium power
in the microwave. Season and serve with
slices of bread and butter, which can be used
to sop up the left-over 'soup'. This dish can
also be cooked for 6 to 7 hours in your
slow-cooker.

Trout

Scotland is renowned for several varieties of trout including sea, brown and rainbow. Whatever your preference, trout can be grilled or baked for a special meal. Allow one trout per person.

Make sure the fish is clean by washing it under the tap, and drying off most of the water with a kitchen towel. Slash the surface of the skin and rub in a little butter or oil.

You can grill trout on either the top of the rack or the base of the grill pan, for about 4 to 5 minutes each side. Just before the second side is ready, coat the top of the fish with flaked almonds. Serve with a salad garnish.

Alternatively, trout may be baked in a conventional oven. Wrap each fish in foil and place in an ovenware dish. Bake for about 35 minutes in a moderate oven, and serve as above. For cooking in the microwave, wrap the tail in foil until the last minute of cooking, and cook on medium power for 4 to 6 minutes. Trout vary considerably in size, but as a guide, the times quoted here are for fish of about 300 g (8/10 oz) each.

Traditionally, trout is served head and all. Eat it by flaking the flesh off one side, then you will be able to peel off the backbone to reach the underside.

Kipper Paté

Ingredients

250 g (8 oz) kippers, or broken kippers
small pack of Philadelphia cheese *or* 225 g
    (7 oz) cottage cheese
knob of butter
1 tablespoon lemon juice
black pepper

Method

Slowly melt the butter over a very low heat,
or in a covered dish in the microwave. Add
the kippers, lemon juice and black pepper,
and gently heat through, for about 8 to 10
minutes on the top of a cooker, or 4 minutes
on low/medium power in the microwave.

Remove from the heat, and stir in the cheese.
Blend the mixture in your food processor or
blender, and spoon into individual rame-
kins, a large paté dish or individual scallop
shells.

Kipper paté is delicious served as a light
lunch with salad and crusty bread, or with
garnish as a starter.

Kippers

A kipper is a smoked herring, still with the skin on its back. They are a beautiful golden brown in colour, and have a very distinctive and delicious taste and aroma. You can buy them in most fish shops, although super-markets stock them packed for convenience. Kippers are best if they are very lightly grilled (about 5 minutes) with a knob of butter on top, and some black pepper. Go easy on the salt, as they are quite salty themselves from the smoking process. They can also be done in the microwave at full power for around 3 minutes for 2 to 3 fish, or, if they are in 'boil-in-the-bag' packages, they can be dropped, bag and all, into boiling water. Cook as directed on the pack.

Serve on hot buttered toast.

Kippers are tasty any time, but are a particular favourite at breakfast.

Arbroath Smokies
(smoked haddock)

Arbroath, situated on the east coast between
Dundee and Montrose, is famous for its
industry of smoking whole (cleaned)
haddock. Unlike the kipper, the flesh of the
fish retains its white colour because the skin
acts as a protection. To serve smokies hot,
dot them with butter, cover the dish with foil,
and heat in a moderate oven. The best way
to appreciate their full flavour, however, is to
eat them just as they are (they are cooked,
after all) with a salad.

Many people go to Arbroath to buy the
smokies straight from the smoking sheds, but
it can be too great a temptation to take them
down to the beach and eat them there and
then!

Remember, smokies are sold in pairs,
although one is generally enough even for
healthy appetites.

Finnan Haddock

Finnan haddies come from the east coast of Scotland, originally from the village of Finnan, some miles south of Aberdeen in the Mearns. They are noted for their own distinctive smoked flavour, quite different from their nearby cousin, the Arbroath smokie. The smokie is whole, with white flesh and copper skin, whereas the haddie is split, and the flesh smoked to a golden yellow colour.

Finnan haddies can be grilled with a knob of butter, or lightly poached without the skin, which shows the unusual marks of 'St Peter's thumbprints' by which they can be easily recognised.

They are also used as the basis for cullen skink (see p 12), a well known and much loved Scottish soup, and can be cooked in milk for a tasty but easy meal.

Kedgeree

Ingredients

250 g (8 oz) smoked haddock
1 small chopped onion
25 g (1 oz) butter
150 g (6 oz) cooked long grain rice
2 chopped hard-boiled eggs
salt and pepper
parsley
a little milk
chopped tomatoes, *or* green beans *or* peas

Method

Cook the fish lightly for 5 minutes on top of the cooker or for 2 minutes in the microwave, then flake it. Melt the butter and gently cook the onion. Cook the rice as directed. Brown rice takes longer than white to cook. Drain the rice and add to the other ingredients. Cook until the kedgeree is heated thoroughly (about 10 minutes on a slow heat on the cooker, and about 4 minutes in the microwave).

Kedgeree can be kept hot for a short time in a very low oven or hostess trolley, but becomes heavy and congealed quite quickly.

VEGETABLE DISHES

Colcannon
(mashed cabbage and potatoes)

Ingredients

1 finely chopped green cabbage
1.5 kg (3 lb) boiled potatoes without their
 jackets

Method

Melt about 25 g (1 oz) butter or margarine in
a pot, or dish if you are using a microwave.
Add the chopped cabbage and cook for
about 10 minutes on the top of a cooker over
a low heat, or about 4 minutes, covered, in
the microwave. Add the hot boiled potatoes, pepper, salt and a lump of butter to
taste, and mash the cabbage and potatoes
together.

For convenience you can use cold mashed
potatoes if you have some left over from a
previous meal.

Colcannon freezes well and reheats easily,
covered, in the microwave. It is a colourful
addition to meat and vegetarian meals, but is
a really tasty snack on its own.

Minty Peas

Ingredients

500 g (1 lb) fresh or frozen peas
butter
chopped mint

Method

Cook the peas as quickly as possible to retain their flavour and colour. Peas are best cooked in a covered bowl for 8 to 10 minutes on full power in the microwave, or dropped into boiling water for 5 or so minutes then drained, or in a vegetable steamer for about 8 minutes if you are cooking on top of the stove. Mix the butter and the mint through the peas.

Some people like to add a teaspoon of sugar to the peas while they are cooking.

Peas keep well in a hostess trolley for up to a couple of hours.

Kale

Ingredients

large bunch of kale
a little butter

Method

Wash and chop the kale and drop it into boiling water or cook in a vegetable steamer, both for about 10 minutes. If you do not have a vegetable steamer, you can easily rig one up by using a wire sieve suspended over boiling water in a pot with a lid, although some steam does escape. Drain and dry the kale and toss in butter and black pepper.

Kale is rich in iron and is very easy to grow as it is a very sturdy vegetable used to the Scottish winter.

Chappit Tatties
(mashed potatoes)

Ingredients

3 medium-sized potatoes per person
50 g (2 oz) butter
a little milk

Method

Peel and rough chop the potatoes, and boil for 20 to 25 minutes, or for 5 minutes on full pressure in a pressure cooker. You can cook them in the microwave, but somehow they do not mash as well as when they are cooked on the top of the stove.

Drain and dry the potatoes, and mash with the milk and butter. Some people like them not completely mashed but with lumps in them. Add white pepper to taste. If you like a crispy top, put the tatties in an oven-proof dish, dot with butter and place in a hot oven or under the grill until the top begins to go brown.

If you are preparing a dinner, you can make chappit tatties well in advance and reheat in the oven or microwave. They retain their flavour and appearance even after a couple of hours in a hostess trolley and freeze well.

Serve with haggis, meat or mince. You can use any left-over tatties for shepherd's pie.

Mashed Neeps
(mashed turnips)

Turnip, in Scotland, is the large purple vegetable with the orange flesh, but many people outside Scotland call this a swede.

Ingredients
1 medium to large-sized turnip
50 g (2 oz) butter

Method

Peel the turnip, making sure that you take off both skins, the purple one on the outside and the greenish-white one underneath. Rough chop the turnip and drop it into boiling salted water. Boil for 25 minutes or cook on full pressure in the pressure cooker for 5 minutes. Drain and dry the turnip and mash with the butter and white pepper to taste.

Serve with haggis or corned beef.

Clapshot
(mashed potatoes and turnips)

Ingredients

1.5 kg (3 lb) potatoes
1 medium-sized turnip
50 g (2 oz) butter

Method

Peel and roughly chop the turnip and the potatoes and place in a large pot of salted boiling water. Boil for 25 minutes, then drain and dry them. You can cook them more quickly in the pressure cooker at full pressure for 5 minutes. Mash the potatoes and turnip together with 50 g (2 oz) butter and black pepper to taste.

Clapshot is really tasty with haggis or any meat. It freezes well, and can be frozen in single portions which can be popped in the microwave for a quick tasty snack.

PUDDINGS

Cranachan
(cream dessert)

Ingredients

100 g (4 oz) toasted coarse oatmeal
500 ml (1 pint) double cream
250 g (½ lb) raspberries *or* brambles
    (blackberries)

Method

Lightly whip the cream, and fold in the toasted oatmeal and the fruit. For a tipsy version of this, you can soak the fruit in Drambuie before adding it to the cream. Scatter toasted oatmeal on top, and chill before serving.

Iris's Trifle

Ingredients

1 Swiss roll or sponge fingers
3 dessertspoons sherry
custard powder
milk
1 strawberry jelly
whipped double cream

Method

Using the sliced Swiss roll or sponge fingers, cover the bottom of a large dessert dish, and pour on the sherry so that the sponge is wet, but not soggy. Drain the fruit, but keep the juice to make the jelly later, and spoon on a layer of fruit on top of the sponge. Make the custard according to the directions on the packet (a packet of pouring custard is ideal also) and pour on top of the fruit to form a layer about 2 to 3 cm (1 inch) thick. Allow the custard to set, and in the meantime melt the jelly, using the reserved juice and boiling water. When the jelly is cool, but still liquid, cover the custard with a layer of jelly, again 2 to 3 cm (1 inch) thick. When the jelly is set firmly, spread a thick layer of whipped cream on top and decorate with vermicelli, chocolate drops or cherries.

Rice Pudding

Ingredients

250 g (8 oz) short grain rice
100 g (4 oz) sugar
½ litre (1 pint) milk

Method

Put all the ingredients into a pan and gently bring to the boil. Lightly simmer for 20 to 25 minutes, and serve hot or cold topped with a spoonful of jam or tinned fruit.

Scotch broth followed by rice pudding makes a tasty lunch for people who are fortunate enough to get home at lunch time. You can even leave each dish cooked and waiting to be reheated in the microwave.

Steam Pudding

Ingredients

100 g (4 oz) self-raising flour
100 g (4 oz) butter
100 g (4 oz) sugar
1 beaten egg
a little milk
fresh rhubarb or apples

Method

Cream the butter and the sugar, and blend in the flour and the egg, adding a little milk if necessary to form a soft mixture. Lightly grease a metal steamer with a tightly fitting lid, and chop the fruit into the bottom. Cover with sugar to taste, and top with the sponge mixture. Seal the steamer, and drop into a pan of boiling water. Cover this with the lid, and boil gently for 25 to 30 minutes.

Serve with milk for a tasty winter pudding.

Clootie Dumpling
(fruit dumpling)

Ingredients

500 g (1 lb) self-raising flour
100 g (4 oz) sugar
75 g (3 oz) butter or margarine
25 g (1 oz) shredded suet
1 teaspoon mixed spice
1 teaspoon ginger
500 g (1 lb) mixed fruit
1 beaten egg
1 tablespoon treacle
1 tablespoon syrup
milk to mix

Method

Mix together the sugar and the flour, and rub in the suet and the butter. Stir in the fruit. Make a well, and gradually add the egg, treacle and syrup (use a spoon dipped in boiling water for each of these). Add a little milk to make a stiff dough.

Put a large pan of water on to boil, and place a plate on the bottom of the pan to prevent the pudding sticking while it is cooking. Take the white cloth, or 'cloot', and scald it in boiling water. Quickly lay it out on your work surface, and dust generously with flour. Put the mixture on the cloth, and draw all the ends together, making sure there are no leakage points. Tie a piece of string securely round the ends of the cloth. Make sure, however, that you leave space for the pudding to swell. Gently lower the pudding into the boiling water, cover with a lid, and boil gently for about 3 hours, always keeping an eye out that there is enough water to cover the pudding.

After 3 hours, remove the cloth gently, taking care that you do not tear the pudding itself, and dry it in a low oven. This will form a firm skin, which many people like as much as the pudding itself.

Serve with cream, custard or on its own, perhaps scattered with sugar.

For birthdays and Christmas, many cooks wrap silver charms in foil or greaseproof paper and hide these in the pudding before it is cooked. Slices of clootie dumpling are delicious fried for breakfast, even 2 of 3 days after it has been made.

THE CHEESEBOARD

Although not as rich in cheese as her neighbour and European cousins, Scotland has always produced cheese in several varieties. Many of these were produced and eaten locally, and never achieved national fame. Our best-known remain Scottish cheddar, produced as both white and red; Dunlop, again in red or white; Orkney, which is red, white or smoked; and Caboc, which is soft and buttery in taste and texture.

However, that is not to say that cheese-making is on the decrease in Scotland. Indeed, it remains a thriving industry with many new types of cheese being manufactured. These are easily available in most delicatessens in the major cities, and in specialist cheese shops up and down the country.

Crowdie
(sour milk cheese)

Ingredients

left-over milk

Method

Heat the milk very slowly in a double boiler until the milk separates. Suspend a piece of muslin or a muslin bag over a bowl, and pour the mixture through the muslin. The solid curds remaining in the bag should be seasoned with a little salt, and left until the whey has drained off. Press the mixture together in the muslin, and transfer to a storage dish or ramekin.

Crowdie is lovely on its own, but can be made even more interesting with the addition of chopped walnuts, oat flakes or chopped chives on top.

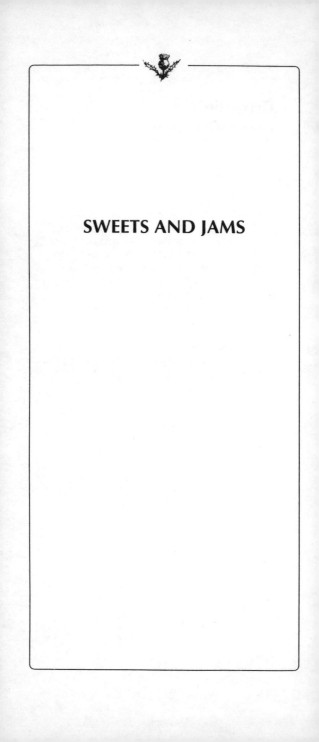

SWEETS AND JAMS

Strawberry or Raspberry Jam (in the microwave)

Ingredients

500 g (1 lb) fruit
700 g (1 lb 6 oz) sugar
dash of lemon juice

Method

Heat the berries in a large uncovered bowl for 4 to 6 minutes until the fruit is soft. Stir in the sugar gradually and gently so that the berries do not break up too much. Cook on full power for 10 to 12 minutes until the setting point is reached. (Test for this by putting a teaspoonful of hot juice on a saucer. It will cool quickly in the refrigerator, and you can see whether it is set by tilting the saucer).

Jam from the microwave is delicious because the fruit does not get bashed to bits by the traditional boiling process. Try the jam with hot pancakes or fresh bread, or on ice cream for an unusual dessert.

Marmalade

Ingredients

1.5 kg (3 lb) Seville oranges
up to 2 litres (4 pints) water
1.5 kg (3 lb) sugar

Method

Pare off and shred the rind from the oranges. Use only half of this for marmalade to suit the majority of tastes, or add a little more for a stronger orange flavour.

Simmer the rind in 250 ml (½ pint) water for 25 to 30 minutes. Rough chop the oranges, and remove the pith and the stones.

Bring the sugar and 1.5 litres (3 pints) water to the boil, and add the orange flesh, the rind and water mixture. Simmer for 20 to 30 minutes, when the marmalade should set when tested. Pour into glass jars, and seal these when the mixture is cold.

The story goes that marmalade was developed to tempt Mary Queen of Scots' appetite when she was ill. Many of her court spoke French, and the name is said to have come from the phrase 'Marie est malade .

Treacle Toffee

Ingredients

250 ml (just over ½ pint) water
100 g (4 oz) butter
500 g (1 lb) brown sugar
50 g (2 oz) syrup
150 g (6 oz) treacle

Method

Gently melt the butter in a heavy-based pan on the top of the cooker. Add the water, and gradually add the sugar until it is completely melted. Stir in the treacle and the syrup, bring to the boil, and boil quickly for about 15 minutes. Take care – the mixture is very hot! Pour into a greased baking tray, and while still warm, score into squares. Leave until completely cold.

Treacle toffee is very moreish, so remember the high calories, weight-watchers. It also sticks delightfully to your teeth, but you can break it into small bite-sized pieces if you wish to eat it elegantly!

Tablet

Ingredients

1 kg (2 lb) white sugar
350 ml (¾ pint) milk
50 g (2 oz) butter
pinch of cream of tartar
1 large spoonful of syrup
vanilla essence

Method

Put all the ingredients (except the vanilla essence) in a pot, adding the syrup from a hot spoon, and melt *very slowly* until the mixture is a thick consistency and light brown in colour. Beat in a little vanilla essence, then pour into a shallow buttered tray, and leave until cool. Score into squares, and gorge yourself when the tablet is cold if you can wait long enough! Tablet is very moreish so take care if you are counting calories.

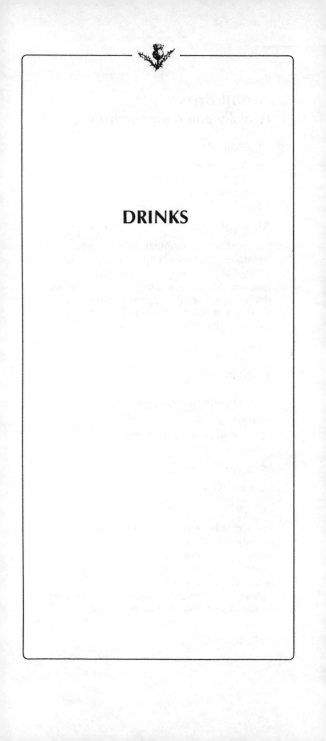

DRINKS

Atholl Brose
(whisky and oatmeal drink)

Ingredients

250 g (8 oz) fine oatmeal
250 g (8 oz) clear runny honey
1 cup cold water
1 litre (2 pints) whisky

Method

Stir together the oatmeal, honey and water.
(Remember, honey comes off the spoon
easily if the spoon is dipped in boiling water
first). Slowly add the whisky and then whisk
the mixture until it froths. Pour into a bottle
and cork it tightly. The mixture is ready for
drinking after a couple of days.

Toddy

Ingredients (for one person)

measure of whisky
1 teaspoon of sugar or honey
a little boiling water

Method

Pour the whisky into a glass and add sugar
and boiling water to taste.

Traditionally, a toddy should be stirred with
a silver spoon, but even if you use a spoon
made of a more modern material (not
plastic, it melts!) a toddy makes you feel
better if you are cold or feel the sniffles
coming on. However, an excuse is not an
essential ingredient in having a toddy.

'Lamb's Milk'

Ingredients (for one person)

1 part whisky
2 parts cold fresh milk

Method

Mix together the whisky and milk. 'Lamb's milk' is delicious – it tastes like an interesting milkshake. Some people claim it is a cure for a hangover – but beware, although it tastes fairly harmless, it can end up giving you one.

A Hogmanay Pick Me Up

Ingredients (for one person)

1 egg
1 tablespoon white sugar
1 tablespoon whisky or pale sherry
milk

Method

Break the egg into a bowl and whisk vigorously. Add the sugar and a little milk, and whisk until the sugar is dissolved. Add the alcohol and pour the mixture into a glass and top up with milk.

Stir this until the milk is mixed through and drink up!

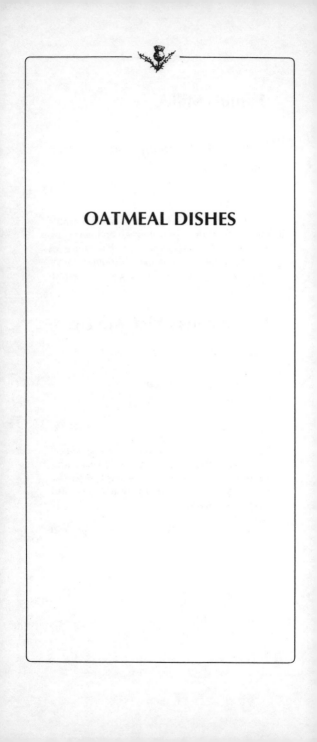

OATMEAL DISHES

Skirlie
(oatmeal savoury)

Ingredients

250 g (8 oz) roast beef dripping
2 onions, finely chopped
up to 500 g (1 lb) fine oatmeal

Method

Melt the dripping in a pan and fry the onions until brown. Stir in the oatmeal until it is thoroughly mixed through the onion.

Skirlie is a lovely 'extra' to mince and tatties, although it stands on its own as a starter or a snack.

Oatcakes

Ingredients

500 g (1 lb) oatmeal
150 g (6 oz) roast beef dripping
some water

Method

Heat the dripping until just melted and stir in the oatmeal. Add enough water to make a stiff dough. Take a dessertspoon of the mixture and squash it together in the palm of your hands – rub your hands in flour first! Now flatten the oatcake out on a floured board, and repeat the process with the rest of the mixture.

There are two ways to cook the oatcakes. You can place them on a greaseproof baking tray and bake them in a hot oven (225°C) until brown. Alternatively, if you have a girdle or cast iron frying-pan, you can cook them lightly on each side. Both ways are successful – the oven method gives a softer oatcake than those done on the top of the stove.

Porridge

Ingredients (for two people)

100 g (4 oz) oatmeal
½ litre (1 pint) water
salt to taste

Method

Soak the oatmeal overnight. Using the same water, bring gently to the boil, adding more water as the mixture begins to thicken and stick to the pot. Simmer for 10 to 15 minutes.

Porridge is a tasty supper dish, when you do not want anything too sweet or heavy. (Coarse oatmeal tends to have a nutty flavour, while fine oatmeal is very subtle). Serve it with milk or cream, or eat the porridge on its own, with salt or sugar.

Traditionally, shepherds out tending their sheep would make enough porridge to last a week, keep it in a special drawer in their bothie and cut a slice for sustenance each day.

Porridge
(in the microwave)

Ingredients

250 g (8 oz) quick-cook porridge oats
200 ml (½ pint) hot water
sprinkling of salt

Method

Heat the salted water in the microwave until it boils. Put the oatmeal in a large bowl (remember the oatmeal will swell) and stir in the water. Cook on full power for 4 to 5 minutes; stir again and allow a couple of minutes' standing time.

Some people are horrified at the thought of eating porridge with sugar and milk – but then it is not very traditional to cook porridge in the microwave either!

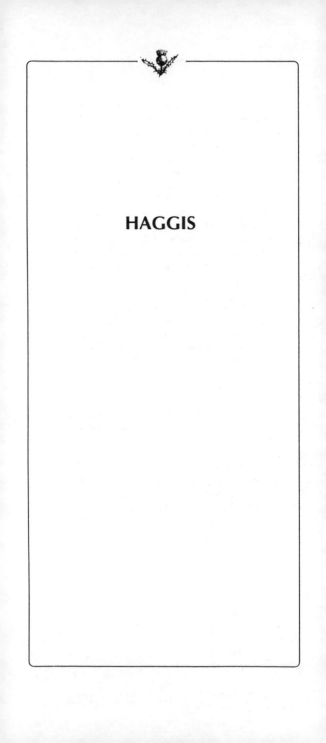

HAGGIS

Contrary to all rumours, haggis is not a Scottish hillside creature, but a well-loved dish made from the heart, lights and liver of a sheep. These are parboiled and then minced with suet, onions and oatmeal. The mixture is packed into the stomach bag of a sheep, which is sewn up, and boiled for 4 to 5 hours. The haggis can then be reheated and served with chappit tatties and butter. Few people make their own haggis nowadays, as the basic ingredients are not normally accessible to the modern cook. Haggis can, however, be easily bought in butchers and supermarkets.

In the same culinary family as haggis, black and white pudding are firm favourites with Scots all over the world. White pudding is made from oatmeal and onions, while black pudding is made from blood with suet, oatmeal and onions. The ingredients for white puddings are wrapped in skin to form a sausage shape which is then reheated in boiling water, and served with butter. Black pudding is baked and served in slices which are fried or grilled, for breakfast.

Each of these puddings is a common feature of most Scottish families' meals, and is served up and down the country in fish and chip shops as a 'pudding supper'.

BREAD AND CAKES

Shortbread

Ingredients

250 g (8 oz) plain flour
125 g (5 oz) rice flour (or ground rice)
100 g (4 oz) caster sugar
250 g (8 oz) Scottish butter

Method

Blend together the dry ingredients, and rub in the butter until the dough resembles shortcrust pastry. Place on a board floured with rice flour, and knead gently for a short while until the dough is smooth. Shape the dough into rounds, or cut into wedges or small rounds with a pastry cutter. For square biscuits, flatten the dough into a flat baking tray, and score the top.

Place the shortbread on a flat baking tray lined with greaseproof paper, and bake in a moderate oven until golden brown.

Black Bun
(rich fruit cake with pastry)

Ingredients

Fruit:
500 g (1 lb) dark raisins
500 g (1 lb) light raisins
1 kg (2 lb) currants
225 g (7 oz) chopped almonds
225 g (7 oz) brown sugar
½ teaspoon cinnamon
½ teaspoon ginger
225 g (7 oz) chopped candied peel
1 beaten egg
milk

Pastry:
500 g (1 lb) flour
125 g (5 oz) butter
½ teaspoon baking soda
buttermilk to mix

Method

Make the pastry first by rubbing the butter into the flour and baking soda, then adding enough buttermilk to make the pastry into a workable consistency. Roll out the pastry very thinly, then line a 1 kilo rectangular greased baking tray with it, setting aside enough to cover the top.

Put all the fruit, nuts and peel into a bowl, rub through the flour and baking soda, and add enough egg and milk to mix into a stiff dough. Put the fruit mixture into the lined tin. Place the pastry cover on top and make sure that the sides are joined. Brush with egg or milk to give a nice glaze.

The only way to cook black bun is to bake it in a moderate oven for 3½ to 4 hours.

Seed Cake

Ingredients

100 g (4 oz) butter
100 g (4 oz) sugar
2 eggs
1 dessertspoon whisky
150 g (6 oz) self-raising flour
1 teaspoon baking powder
1 dessertspoon caraway seeds

Method

Cream the butter and sugar. In two other separate bowls beat together the eggs and the whisky, and blend the dry ingredients. Add the egg mix and the dry ingredients alternately to the butter and sugar, taking care that the mixture does not curdle. Pour into a greased and lined 20 cm (8 inch) cake tin, and bake for 40 to 45 minutes at 175°C.

Gingerbread

Ingredients

250 g (8 oz) butter
250 g (8 oz) brown sugar
250 g (8 oz) treacle
3 teaspoons ground ginger
500 g (1 lb) self-raising flour
milk to mix

Method

Cream the butter and sugar, and gradually add the treacle. Add the dry ingredients with enough milk to make a soft mixture. Pour this into a lined and greased cake tin, and bake at 175°C for 1 to 1½ hours. Gingerbread can be baked in a round or in a shallow square cake tin, when it can be cut into squares for serving.

Gingerbread is delicious on its own, as a cake, or sliced and spread with butter. For a tasty pudding during the winter, serve it with hot pouring custard.

Dundee Cake
(fruit cake)

Ingredients

250 g (8 oz) butter
250 g (8 oz) sugar
4 beaten eggs
250 g (8 oz) flour
500 (1 lb) mixed fruit
125 g (5 oz) mixed peel
100g (4 oz) blanched almonds (reserve a little for decoration)

Method

Cream the sugar and the butter, and add the eggs, a little at a time, taking care that the mixture does not curdle. Gradually add the dry ingredients, using a little milk if the mixture becomes too stiff to work with. Pour into a greased and lined 20 cm (8 inch) cake tin, and scatter the remaining almonds on top. If you are feeling creative you can make a pattern! Bake in a moderate oven for 1½ to 2 hours.

Morning Rolls

Ingredients

500 g (1 lb) plain flour
50 g (2 oz) white lard
1 teaspoon salt
25 g (1 oz) yeast
200 ml (½ pint) milk mixed with a little
    water

Method

Yeast which can be added to the dry ingredients (without having to froth the yeast) is much easier to use. If you prefer to start the yeast mixture separately you will need a teaspoon of sugar and a little warm water.

Sift the flour and salt into a warmed bowl, add the yeast to the dry ingredients, and rub in the lard. Alternatively, rub in the lard to the flour and salt, and add the yeast mixture when frothy.

Use the milk to mix up a soft dough, then cover the bowl with a cloth and leave in a warm place. After about an hour, the dough will have risen. Knead it with your hands, in a food processor or with a dough hook until it is smooth.

Make roll shapes by taking a handful of dough and forming it into a round about the size of a tennis ball. Place these on a greased and floured baking tray. Gently squash the rounds until they are about half their original height, brush with milk and dust with flour. Leave the tray in a warm place for about 20 minutes, then place it in a hot oven for 15 to 20 minutes.

Morning rolls are delicious eaten hot, straight out of the oven.

Potato Scones

Ingredients

500 g (1 lb) warm mashed potatoes
125 g (5 oz) plain flour

Method

Blend the flour into the potatoes, adding a little butter if necessary. Roll or pat out the dough to about 5 mm thick, although you can vary this to taste. Cook the scones on a hot girdle or frying-pan for about 2 minutes each side until brown.

Potato scones are delicious with eggs and bacon for breakfast, or later in the day with tea.

Andrew's Pancakes or Drop Scones

Ingredients

250 g (8 oz) self-raising flour
100 g (4 oz) sugar
pinch of baking powder
a little salt
1 egg
milk to taste

Method

Mix together the dry ingredients and make a well in the centre of the bowl. Drop in the egg, and gradually blend in the flour mixture, adding enough milk to make a smooth creamy mixture. Beat this for a few minutes, and cover the bowl with a cloth. Leave the mixture to stand for about an hour, and do not mix it any more – it is ready for cooking. Drop spoonfuls of the mixture on to a lightly greased hot girdle or frying-pan, and cook for a couple of minutes each side. You know the pancake is ready for turning when it begins to bubble on top.

Pancakes freeze well, and are a great stand-by as a snack or with tea. They are also delicious refried or toasted and served with fried eggs for breakfast.

Girdle Scones

Ingredients

250 (8 oz) self-raising flour
a little salt
50 g (2 oz) butter or margarine
milk

Method

Rub in the butter to the flour and salt, and mix with enough milk to make a stiff dough. Roll or pat out the mixture to a thickness of about 1 cm, and cut into wedges. Cook on a moderately hot girdle or heavy-based frying-pan for about 3 to 4 minutes each side.

Meg's Scones

Ingredients

150 g (6 oz) self-raising flour
50 g (2 oz) sugar
50 g (2 oz) butter or margarine
1 beaten egg
a little milk to mix

Method

Mix the sugar and flour, and rub in the butter or margarine. Add the egg and milk to form a stiff dough, and place the mixture in a floured sandwich tin. Alternatively, pat out the dough on a floured board and cut into rounds or wedges, and place on a floured baking tray. Bake the scones in a hot oven for about 10 to 15 minutes, until golden brown.

The secret of good scones is to mix them up quickly without too much handling. Serve hot with newly-made strawberry jam.

SET MEALS AND
CELEBRATIONS

A Guid Scots Breakfast

Many people still relish a good breakfast to set them up for the day.

Porridge (with or without milk)
Grilled kippers on toast *or*
Grilled bacon with fried eggs, mushrooms and grilled tomatoes, fried pancakes or potato scones
Morning rolls *or* oatcakes and butter
Toast and marmalade

All washed down with good strong tea.

In the past, people with enough money would have two or three courses at breakfast, including meat stews washed down with ales or wine. However, they generally started work very early in the morning, so 'breakfast' was almost the midday meal. It is easy to see that, as hours of working gradually became later, so the main meal of the day slipped backwards to midday.

Dinner, Afternoon Tea and High Tea

Although Scotland is a leader in the field of high technology, many people still stick to the traditional ways of eating. After all, through the years they have proved how convenient they are!

'Dinner' for a lot of people means a two-course meal between 12 noon and 2 pm of soup and a sweet, or soup and a main course. Nowadays many people still speak of their 'dinner', but it is just a snack because people have a three-course meal in the evening after 7pm, a practice which is much more European than Scottish, despite our links with France.

However, many of the gentle ladies of Edinburgh and Glasgow were, and still are, known to meet for afternoon tea in various well-known venues such as Jenners in Edinburgh and Miss Cranston's tea rooms in Glasgow. Thankfully there are many less well-known but just as reliable tea shops which offer excellent service.

High tea takes place between 5 and 7 pm, and is a delightful meal which consists of a main course, generally a mixed grill or fish, with a pot of tea, and a plate of scones and cakes. Many people today still have high tea, but sadly it is a dying feature of Scottish life.

A Christening Piece

The old custom of the christening piece was prevalent up until the late 1930s but is seldom heard of now. When a child was to be baptised in church or in the manse, it was the custom to walk to the church carrying the child in his or her finest clothing. The baby was carried by the godmother, accompanied by the godfather and other relations, all decked out in their 'Sunday best'. The godfather carried a small parcel which he handed to the first person of the opposite sex to the baby they met as they walked. This was a lucky piece and was much sought-after, and most people tried to ensure that the piece was given to a child. The parcel or bag would contain a piece of silver (usually a florin or two shilling coin), an assortment of cakes and sweets, and perhaps an orange or an apple.

Burns Night

All over the world on and around the evening of 25 January each year, Scots and their descendants gather to celebrate the birth of Robert Burns, the famous Scots poet. The proceedings follow a fairly strict pattern, and speakers are chosen to give the toast to the lassies, the recitation of the 'Address to the Haggis', and songs from the varied and prolific works of Robert Burns. The haggis, held high, is escorted in by a man playing the bagpipes – or the pipes as they are known in Scotland – and the assembled company is not served until the haggis on the top table has been skewered at the end of the Address.

A traditional menu for a Burns Supper would include: Scotch broth; haggis with chappit tatties and neeps; trifle; cheese and oatcakes. All washed down with true Scotch whisky.

St Andrew's Night

St Andrew is the patron saint of Scotland. The distinctive blue and white St Andrew's Cross on the Scottish flag is a reminder of the cross upon which St Andrew was himself crucified. His Saint's Day is 30 November. Until recently, all celebrations were confined to the evening, when a 'social' was, and still is, held by the community, religious or political groups, or by groups of friends. A 'social' is an evening event when people get together and have a meal with haggis as the main course, followed by an organised concert, or even better, a series of 'turns' from the assembled company who each do their party piece.

Glaswegians are known for their quick and sharp wit which can reduce even the most sombre member of the company to unrestrained giggles. It is an often repeated maxim amongst Glasgow people, academics to artisans, that 'you should never leave a turn unstoned'.

Recently, 30 November has been a recognised holiday in many regions of Scotland.

Hogmanay

On the last night of the Old Year and the first minutes of the New, Scots prefer to be awake and in their own homes, or with friends. Many nowadays eat early in the evening and see the New Year in with a party, while some leave eating until 10.30 or 11 pm and time it so that they see the New Year in at the end of their meal.

Many of the old traditions live on. Hundreds of young people gather at the Tron Kirk in the Royal Mile in Edinburgh, in the City Square in Dundee, and in various centres up and down the country to welcome in the New Year. In their homes too, many people abandon the vacuum cleaner and sweep the floor, so that the Auld Year is swept out just as the New Year is welcomed in.

After midnight (the first stroke of twelve on the clock), the assembled party wish each other a Happy New Year, most often with a kiss or a hug, and a toast is drunk. Relatives and friends call on each other, in person or by telephone, throughout the early hours of the morning and during the first few days of the New Year. For luck, your 'first foot' (your first visitor after midnight) should be a tall, dark man. When you 'first foot' somebody (that is to visit them for the first time in the first few weeks of the New Year), it is customary to take some shortbread, or a lump of coal, some tea or some token of goodwill. Black bun and seed cake are served in abundance with tea or whisky.